Ancestral Future

Critical South

The publication of this series is supported by the International Consortium of Critical Theory Programs funded by the Andrew W. Mellon Foundation.

Series editors: Natalia Brizuela, Victoria Collis-Buthelezi, and Leticia Sabsay

Leonor Arfuch, *Memory and Autobiography*
Paula Biglieri and Luciana Cadahia, *Seven Essays on Populism*
Aimé Césaire, *Resolutely Black*
Bolívar Echeverría, *Modernity and "Whiteness"*
Diego Falconí Trávez, *From Ashes to Text*
Celso Furtado, *The Myth of Economic Development*
Eduardo Grüner, *The Haitian Revolution*
Ailton Krenak, *Ancestral Future*
Ailton Krenak, *Life Is Not Useful*
Premesh Lalu, *Undoing Apartheid*
Karima Lazali, *Colonia Trauma*
María Pia López, *Not One Less*
Achille Mbembe and Felwine Sarr, *The Politics of Time*
Achille Mbembe and Felwine Sarr, *To Write the Africa World*
Valentin-Yves Mudimbe, *The Scent of the Father*
Pablo Oyarzun, *Doing Justice*
Néstor Perlongher, *Plebeian Prose*
Bento Prado Jr., *Error, Illusion, Madness*
Nelly Richard, *Eruptions of Memory*
Suely Rolnik, *Spheres of Insurrection*
Silvia Rivera Cusicanqui, *Ch'ixinakax utxiwa*
Tendayi Sithole, *The Black Register*
Maboula Soumahoro, *Black is the Journey, Africana the Name*
Dénètem Touam Bona, *Fugitive, Where Are You Running?*

Ancestral Future

Ailton Krenak

Edited by
Rita Carelli

Translated by
Alex Brostoff and Jamille Pinheiro Dias

polity

Originally published in Portuguese as *Futuro Ancestral* © 2022, Ailton Krenak
Published in Brazil by Companhia das Letras, São Paulo. International Rights
Management: Susanna Lea Associates

This English edition © Polity Press, 2024

Polity Press
65 Bridge Street
Cambridge CB2 1UR, UK

Polity Press
111 River Street
Hoboken, NJ 07030, USA

ISBN-13: 978-1-5095-6072-1 – hardback
ISBN-13: 978-1-5095-6073-8 – paperback

A catalogue record for this book is available from the British Library.

Library of Congress Control Number: 2023938506

Typeset in 12.5 on 17 pt Sabon
by Fakenham Prepress Solutions, Fakenham, Norfolk NR21 8NL
Printed and bound in Great Britain by TJ Books Ltd, Padstow, Cornwall

The publisher has used its best endeavours to ensure that the URLs for external websites
referred to in this book are correct and active at the time of going to press. However, the
publisher has no responsibility for the websites and can make no guarantee that a site will
remain live or that the content is or will remain appropriate.

Every effort has been made to trace all copyright holders, but if any have been overlooked
the publisher will be pleased to include any necessary credits in any subsequent reprint or
edition.

For further information on Polity, visit our website:
politybooks.com

Contents

Introduction: The Affective Alliances of Translation

A Time for Kinship

A defense of life emerges in this paradoxically titled book. In *Ancestral Future*, Ailton Krenak elucidates how humanity must amplify the sounds of the rivers and the rhythms of the Earth over and against the thrum of the metropolis and its mechanization of life. Necrocapitalism, he shows, systematically extracts our sense of presence, rendering us disconnected from the power of life. Both labor and land are ruthlessly exploited for profit, reinforcing the oppressive power structures dominating our world. The future, as necrocapitalism imagines it, reproduces a system of disposability that reaches beyond the human and impacts other forms of life. The act of fixating on a hypothetical and idealized future only intensifies the sensation of time accelerating beyond our control. Ailton, as he would be referred to in Brazil, shows us how constantly looking to the future causes us to neglect the present, which has ramifications that surpass human suffering and extend across the entire ecosystem, as our planet is increasingly subjected to the pressures of this rapid acceleration. The relentless pursuit of an imagined future has led to devastating effects on biodiversity, climate change, and the environment writ large.

But Ailton refuses to be bound by the crises of our times and the capitalist bondage of the future. Instead, he moves away from the dehumanizing automation of modern urban existence; he rejects the conditions of the Capitalocene. Within this seemingly bleak reality, he perceives an anti-teleological future, one that breaks free from the logics of accumulation. After all, Indigenous understandings of time differ significantly from linear concepts of progress. For many Indigenous communities, time is not experienced as a succession of isolated events, but, rather, as a continuous and interconnected cycle. Indigenous temporalities acknowledge the seasonal cycles of nature and the movements of celestial bodies, which serve as essential references for daily practices such as planting, harvesting, hunting, grieving, and healing. Ancestral memory is passed down through oral traditions that impart such values and principles, which guide social and political organization. In this context, time matters not only as it is measured by the clock and divided into hours, minutes, and seconds, but, more significantly, for lived experience.

For Ailton, the ever-shifting form of rivers reflects this nonlinear temporality. Through the lens of the water, this understanding of time leads Ailton to propose that if there is a conceivable future, it is at once ancestral and also present in the here and now. He urges us to draw wisdom from ancient knowledges embedded in nonhuman forms of life. This philosophy of time embraces the interconnectedness of beings and suggests that the future is rooted in ancestral knowledge. In his words, "rivers, those beings that have always inhabited different worlds, are the ones that suggest to me that if there is a future to imagine, it is ancestral, since it is already present." Ailton's philosophy of time thus relies on a perception of rivers as living beings that have traversed different worlds and taken different forms. By restoring "subjectivity to rivers and mountains," as Rita Carelli writes in her afterword, Ailton highlights their enduring presence, suggesting that rivers carry time's cyclical and interconnected nature as they flow. Carelli emphasizes the delicate task of conveying the currents of Ailton's flowing thoughts.

As translators, we likewise seek to amplify the ways in which Ailton has become a voice for the injured rivers – not by romanticizing them and praising their pristine waters, but by bemoaning the devastation and toxicity the Capitalocene has inflicted on them. Ailton emphasizes the lessons that ancient rivers teach us and how they may guide us toward enhancing our existence without harming other forms of life. The history plotted in *Ancestral Future*, however, also acknowledges how major rivers such as the Nile in Egypt and the Ganges in India have been instrumentalized in the rise of civilization and the resultant onslaught of catastrophe. Near his village in the Brazilian state of Minas Gerais, the Doce River, as Ailton describes, has fallen into a coma from catastrophic mining contamination caused by the collapse of local dams. Ailton does not normalize these socio-environmental calamities; instead, he confronts them head on, leading the way toward a future that can only come to be if it is ancestral.

Ancestral wisdom, according to Ailton, has never existed as a fixed point in the past, but has always been a creation of the future; that is, an ethical mode of knowledge production that emphasizes how we build, inhabit, and create existence on and with the Earth. *Ancestral Future*'s approach to temporality and the futures it makes possible thus relies on forms of kinship that extend beyond the human. By recasting our existence in constellation with nonhuman life, Ailton urges us to break free from the shackles of exploitation and collectively work toward a more just and sustainable future. This perspective is deeply entwined with other beings who cohabit time–space with us, beings with whom Indigenous peoples recognize a relationship of interdependence. As such, the phrase "we-river, we-mountains, we-earth" conceives of a "we" that signifies an entanglement with these entities, an interdependence that ranges beyond mere observation or appreciation. Opening oneself to experiencing the world from the perspective of the rivers, the mountains, and the Earth enables a departure from the confines of anthropocentrism, in which humanity understands nature as separate and subordinate to itself. Indeed, Indigenous temporality awaits the time in which all living beings are in constellation with each other – a perspective that the exploitative speed of capitalist time violates viciously and repeatedly.

Reforesting the Imagination

Skeletons of iron and concrete, scaffolding pervaded by industry, structures that decimate forests, dispossess communities, and corral the commons: this is how Ailton characterizes "the prosthesis that cities have become worldwide." If, on the one hand, the prosthetic metaphor alludes to biomedical means of life support, it also, on the other, refers to technological advances that blight the Earth by wiping out nonrenewable resources. In "Cities, Pandemics, and Other Gadgets," Ailton rails against the historical opposition between the city and the forest, an opposition multiplied by capitalism's ever-encroaching investment in urbanity. For Ailton, the urban order is not just an architecture of enclosure, but a culture of sanitation that transforms earth into dirt. Worse yet, the modern metropolis makes no space for *o comum* (the commons). While our translation of "the commons" nods toward an array of notions endemic to Western philosophy from Baruch Spinoza to Fred Moten, Ailton's conceptualization conjures a vast sense of that which is shared or common among peoples, be it culture, space, or forms of life. And yet, rather than make space for human and nonhuman bodies to share, urban culture breeds privatization, promising a prolongation of individualist and identitarian life through technological means.

After all, the very concept of *cidadania* (citizenship) contains the word *cidade* (city). Citizenship, in other words, is founded on the city; urbanity produces national belonging. Conversely, *florestania*, a word that wonderfully defies translation, manifests how citizenship exceeds urban prerogatives. Containing the word *floresta* (forest), *florestania* expresses the ability to organize and advocate not only for the forest, but for waterways and for biodiversity and life beyond the cityscape. In Ailton's understanding, *florestania* conveys the struggle to expand the space for exercising citizenship beyond urban settings and to extend human rights to the residents of the forest and the water. Pushing back against the compulsory sanitation of urban order imposed by pavement and private property, by the police and the prison industrial complex, *florestania* flowers in defense of the forest and the life forms that thrive there.

And yet, as deforestation continues to devastate Indigenous territories, Ailton's approach to urbanity rejects Western logics that divide the city and the forest. On the contrary, he calls on us "to reforest our imagination," and, in turn, "reconnect with a poetics of urbanity that restores the power of life." How, in other words, can we contest the privatization and sanitization of urban spheres that capitalize on cloistering? What can we learn from the grammars of a yard growing wild? "How," asks Ailton, "can we make the forest exist within us, within our homes, within our yards? ... How can we convert industrial urban fabric into natural urban fabric, centering nature and transforming cities from within?" Such questions refuse to rhyme with neoliberal sustainability campaigns; instead, they press on, reforesting our imaginations in order to reforest the world.

Lessons in Longing

Diverging from linear progress narratives that peg moral imperatives to crisis-mongering, Ailton's approach acknowledges the ways in which dominant modes of knowledge production are conditioned by histories of genocide, dispossession, and assimilation. When he speaks of "the words 'mold,' 'shape,' 'form,' 'format,' etc.," he expresses how "these words prune spirits." To be subjected to formal education, in other words, is to rob a being of its subjectivity and breed futures dominated by "winners and losers," futures doomed to harm other life forms.

What would education look like were it not bound within the buildings of the state? *Ancestral Future* isn't about just temporality, but also spatiality, and Ailton walks us through modes of schooling that rely not only on intergenerational exchange, but do so beyond the conformist confines of institutionalized machination. Ailton speaks to the lessons one learns in friction with nature, which leads to a reevaluation of education writ large. He advocates for education that proffers experience free from dogma, speciesism, and sanitarianism, all of which trap us indoors. Such entrapment, he shows, renders the outdoors unclean, while discouraging us from connecting with soil, plants, seeds, and animals.

He reminds us, by contrast, of how "pedagogical experience can be achieved at the shore of a stream, on a slab of stone, anywhere. It's a group effort to make a collective investigation." Brazil's National Plan for Indigenous Education (*Plano Nacional de Educação Escolar Indígena*) enables Indigenous communities to design and implement schooling with respect to that group's knowledges. Imagine if, as Ailton argues, school was not a building in which an individual developed, but an exchange that focused on collective experience. What would be learned wouldn't be about molding someone into something, but, rather, about embracing a sense of longing.

How does one learn "to long for worlds"? As translators, we learn the lesson of longing for worlds repeatedly: with each turn of phrase, an exercise in interpretive possibility; with each sentence, an education in the craft of conveying cultural context. Not only has translating *Life Is Not Useful* and *Ancestral Future* proffered an education beyond borders and walls, but, as a critical and creative praxis, our collaborative labor as co-translators has been in the service of galvanizing and energizing the very kinds of *alianças afetivas* (affective alliances) that Ailton conceptualizes. *Afeto*, after all, connotes "warmth," "endearment," and "esteem." Beyond the English-language notion of "affect" or "affection," *afeto* is tender; it is dear and it is fond.

As we make affective bonds, so too do those bonds remake us. We conjugate and we are conjugated by the radical inequalities that constellate us. Translation is multidirectional in this sense: as we translate, we are translated. An affective alliance, in its esteem for "an intrinsic otherness in each person, in each being," does not skim over or dissolve difference, but, on the contrary, "introduces a kind of radical inequality." Like Ailton, we, too, are forced to pause and remove our footwear, paying heed to what transpires in that dizzying, barefoot dance between worlds. And in that constellation, we find ourselves taking part in the flux of signification. As translation works to bridge different timescales through language, it plays a significant part in shaping our cultural imaginaries. Just as Ailton emphasizes the interconnection between time and rivers as dynamic entities, so too do translators face the challenge of preserving the fluidity of a given text while adapting it to new linguistic and cultural contexts.

Translators are in constellation not only with the author, text, and reader, but with languages; and in constellating languages, we construct and disrupt relationships to the very experience of meaning-making. Unlike being "in conversation" or "in community," being "in constellation" highlights our interdependence on each other, as well as on forms of life beyond the human – both visible and invisible to the human eye. Ailton advocates for a form of education that enables the perception of oneself as belonging to a collective, which transforms the world into precisely "where we are now." This is why "Education has nothing to do with the future," as he explains, "After all, the future is imaginary, and education is an experience that has to be real." A collective subject thus senses a constellation between the self and the organism that is earth. A collective subject shares the world and that which is within and beyond it.

In solidarity with *Ancestral Future*'s anticapitalist and anti-anthropocentric call to action, translation, we wager, participates in such an education. As climate catastrophe crescendos, our cultural imaginaries are tested and translation emerges on the global stage as a political means of recasting how we relate to and care for human and nonhuman forms of life. We hope that this work welcomes you into constellation with such affective alliances.

Alex Brostoff and Jamille Pinheiro Dias

In this invocation of ancestral time, I see a group of seven or eight children paddling in a canoe:

The children rowed in a rhythmic manner, and everyone touched their oars on the water's surface with great tranquility and harmony: they were living out their childhoods in the sense of coming closer to ancient times, as their people, the Yudja, refer to it. One of them, an elder, as he was describing his experience, spoke up: "Our parents say we're already getting closer to how things used to be."

I thought it was beautiful that those children yearned for what their ancestors had taught them, and that they valued it in the present moment. In my recollection, these boys are not seeking a prospective idea of time or anything like that, but rather what will happen right here, in this ancestral place that is their territory within the rivers.

Greetings to the Rivers

The rivers, those beings that have always inhabited different worlds, are the ones that suggest to me that if there is a future to imagine, it is ancestral, because it is already present. I like to believe that all those we are able to invoke in the form of becoming are our traveling companions, even if they are immemorable, because the passage of time becomes a distraction in our sensitive observations of the planet. But we are in the Pacha Mama, which has no borders, so it makes no difference whether we are above or below the Rio Grande; we are everywhere, because our ancestors, the river-mountains, are in everything, and I'm sharing the unrestrained wealth of being able to experience these presents with you.

Wherever I have been, whether in Brazil or in other parts of the world, I have paid more attention to the waters than to the urban structures that peer over them, because all our human settlements in Europe, Asia, Africa, and everywhere else have always been drawn to the rivers. A river is a path within a city that allows for movement, despite the fact that it has been some time since people decided to stay put in cities. Children are taught in classrooms that one of the world's earliest civilizations originated in the delta of the Nile River in Egypt, where the river's waters irrigated the banks and provided conditions for agriculture – this civilizing idea. We have always been near water, but it seems that we have learned very little from the language of the rivers. This practice of listening to what the waterways have to say has made me think critically about how cities (especially the big ones) are spreading over the rivers in such an irreverent way that we almost don't show any respect for them anymore.

Our Krenak ancestors would place thirty-, forty-day-old babies in the Watu River, reciting the words, *"Rakandu, nakandu, nakandu, racandu."* There, the children were protected against pests, diseases, and every other possible harm. This river of ours, called the Doce River[1] by the whites, whose waters flow less than a kilometer from the backyard of my house, sings. We listen to its voice and talk to

---

[1] *TR.* The Doce River is located in the southeastern region of Brazil, flowing through the states of Minas Gerais and Espírito Santo.

our river-music when it is quiet at night. We like to thank it because it gives us food and this great water, it broadens our worldviews and makes our lives more meaningful. At night, the river's waters run swiftly and murmurously, and their whispers travel down the rocks to form rapids that make music. At this time, the rock and the water are so wonderfully entangled with us that we can say "we-river, we-mountains, we-earth." We feel so deeply immersed in these beings that we allow ourselves to leave our bodies, this anthropomorphic sameness, and experience other ways of existing. For example, we allow ourselves to be water and feel this incredible power that it has to take different paths.

I also salute the Jequitinhonha and the Mucuri Rivers, which, like Watu, make the long journey to the sea.

In my life, I have had the great blessing of getting my hands and feet wet, and of diving, swimming, tasting and smelling and eating the fish from dozens, maybe hundreds, of streams and rivers. A long time ago, I was able to bathe in the Madeira River.[2] It was my first time entering its waters. It was raining heavily and the river was rough – I enjoyed playing a little, but stayed close to the bank so as not to be

---

[2] *TR.* The Madeira River is located in western Brazil and flows northward through the Brazilian Amazonian states of Rondônia and Amazonas. It is a major tributary of the Amazon River.

swept away by the current. I have never dared to
cross any of these rivers, because I have had friends
who were swept away by the waters. Even smaller
rivers, not those as big as the Branco River, have
a magical force capable of carrying us away. It is
fascinating to think that the great river that gives the
Amazon Basin its name is born from a small stream
in the Andes to form this aquatic world. It carries
many other rivers, but it also carries the water that
the forest itself gives to the clouds, and that the rain
gives back to the Earth in this wonderful cycle in
which the waters of the rivers are those of the sky,
and the waters of the sky are those of the river.

Xingu, Amazonas, Rio Negro, Solimões.[3]

I wasn't surprised when people started talking
about flying rivers.[4] Waterways are capable of
covering long distances, finding new paths, diving
into the Earth, and – why not? – flying. In the Serra
do Divisor,[5] there is the impressive Moa,[6] a kind of

---

[3] TR. The Xingu, Amazonas, Rio Negro, and Solimões are all
located in the Amazon Basin.

[4] TR. Flying rivers are immense volumes of water vapor that
are present over large areas of the Amazon and circulate in
the atmosphere. They originate from the Atlantic Ocean and
precipitate as rain in the Amazon, from where they disperse
throughout the South American continent.

[5] TR. Serra do Divisor is a mountain range located in the
western part of the state of Acre in Brazil, near the border
with Peru.

[6] TR. Moa is a river that flows through the Serra do Divisor

large Paraná River[7] that flows down to the Javari,[8] empties into the Solimões,[9] and, along with waters from Colombia, also reaches the Amazon Basin. Further up from Cruzeiro do Sul, in the middle Juruá, lies the territory of our Ashaninka relatives. Once, I traveled with them up to the headwaters of the river, dragging a canoe because the waters were very low, and I was surprised to find a small stream up there, near the end of Brazil, called Tejo, and couldn't help but think of Fernando Pessoa, who also sang about his river.[10]

National Park and is one of the main tributaries of the Juruá River, which is itself a tributary of the Amazon River.

[7] *TR.* The Paraná River is located in the southern part of Brazil. It forms part of the border between Brazil and Paraguay, as well as between Brazil and Argentina.

[8] *TR.* The Javari River is a tributary of the Amazon River and forms part of the border between Brazil and Peru. The river originates in the Andes Mountains in Peru and flows approximately 820 kilometers eastward before joining the Amazon River near the city of Benjamin Constant in Brazil.

[9] *TR.* The Solimões River is the name given to the section of the Amazon River that begins at the confluence of the Ucayali and Marañón Rivers in Peru and flows through Brazil.

[10] *TR.* Portuguese poet Fernando Pessoa wrote several poems about the Tejo River, also known as the Tagus River, which is an important river that flows through Portugal, including through the capital city of Lisbon. One of Pessoa's most famous poems about the Tejo River is called "Ode Marítima" or "Maritime Ode." He used the heteronym Álvaro de Campos to sign this poem.

Juruá, Jutaí,[11] Javari – children recite this from stilt houses.

Our relatives who live there on the border of Peru and Colombia reside in floating villages, built on platforms above the water. They are people who need the living water, who need the spirits of water present, the poetry it brings to life, and that is why they're called the peoples of the waters. Most people think that life can only be lived on solid ground and can't imagine that there is a part of humanity that finds the completeness of their existence, their culture, their economy, and their sense of belonging in water. In Lake Titicaca, there is an ancient group of people who also live on platforms on the water. There, in that space, everyone is born and dies, raises small animals, and children play. They live in and from the water, that power of life that has been disturbed by the noisy, urban presence of humans, who always want more and, if necessary, build Belo Monte, Tucuruí,[12] dams in every basin to satisfy the

---

[11] *TR.* The Juruá and Jutaí Rivers are both located in the western part of the Brazilian state of Amazonas. They are part of the Amazon Basin.

[12] *TR.* With a construction history steeped in human rights violations, the Belo Monte Dam Complex, which is located on the northern part of the Xingu River in the state of Pará, is the second largest hydroelectric dam in Brazil. Its internationally contested construction has resulted in the displacement of thousands of Indigenous peoples and a grave loss of water access and biodiversity in the affected areas.

infinite thirst of their cities, homes of those who no longer know how to live in the waters and forests. Guaporé,[13] Araguaia,[14] São Francisco.[15] Sometimes I feel more moved by the presence of these rivers than by humans like me. This village where I am located is in the eastern region of Minas Gerais, closer to the sea than to the Central Plateau of Brazil. Here, I am constantly surrounded by the sound of water, including underground rivers, which makes me think of the book *Deep Rivers* by the great Peruvian writer José María Arguedas. In it, the spirit of the water cuts through valleys and mountains, and carries stories and wonders wherever it goes. Arguedas has a fascinating perception of that river that cuts through

With similarly devastating effects, the Tucuruí Dam was constructed on the Tocantins River in the state of Pará in the early 1980s. Its construction caused mass displacement, deforestation, and destruction of the ecosystem.

[13] TR. The Guaporé River flows through Brazil and Bolivia. It originates in the mountains of the state of Mato Grosso in Brazil and flows to the northwest, passing through the Brazilian state of Rondônia before entering Bolivia and eventually joining the Mamoré River.

[14] TR. The Araguaia River flows through the states of Goiás, Mato Grosso, Tocantins, and Pará in Brazil. It starts in the central part of Brazil and flows in a northeastern direction, eventually joining the Tocantins River.

[15] TR. The São Francisco River spans several Brazilian states, including Minas Gerais, Bahia, Pernambuco, Alagoas, and Sergipe. It originates in the state of Minas Gerais and flows northeast, ultimately reaching the Atlantic Ocean.

the Andes, that river capable of carving its way through rocks with great force, and descending in a devastating manner without anyone able to navigate its body because it is such a fierce river. I went to Saint Petersburg once, to the banks of the Neva River, and I must tell you this: during part of the year, this river freezes to such an extent that it is possible to ride a horse on it. As a person from the tropics, I was amazed by that ...

Imagine "riding" the Tapajós,[16] the Madeira, the Tocantins![17]

What intrigues me is that some of these bodies of water manage to outlive us without suffering the humiliation and fractures that others have endured. It must be said that these rivers I evoke here are being mutilated: each one of them has its body scarred by some damage, whether it be from gold panning, large-scale mining, or the wrongful appropriation of the landscape. I find it intriguing that some people find it natural to consider a river sacred as long as it's in India and they can recite

[16] *TR.* The Tapajós River is located in the north-central part of Brazil, flowing through the states of Mato Grosso and Pará. It is a major tributary of the Amazon.

[17] *TR.* The Tocantins River is located in central and northern Brazil. It primarily runs through the states of Tocantins and Pará. The river originates in the state of Goiás. It then flows northward, forming the border between the states of Tocantins and Maranhão before reaching Pará and eventually flowing into the Atlantic Ocean.

the name Ganges in their sleep, even as they dare to plunder the body of the river next to them whose name they don't even know, to cool industrial cycles and commit other absurdities. For more than 2,000 years, human communities have established their villages along the banks of the Tapajós. And today, our Munduruku[18] and Sateré Mawé[19] relatives continue to fight to protect the body of this river from the infrastructural apparatus that the government insists on implementing, as well as from the harassment of mining, logging, and other acts of violence. I heard that in the same region, riverside communities had to stop doing things that nourish their families because the fish are sick. The fish have what is called "black urine." Riverside communities have started to consider raising fish in ponds and fish farms to replace the natural fishing that used to be done in the streams. We're destroying this source of life, food, and abundance.

Unfortunately, in the urban part of São Paulo that the Tietê River traverses, the water has turned into sewage. I don't know how a city can do that;

[18] TR. The Munduruku are a group of approximately 14,000 people who live in the Brazilian Amazon, primarily in the states of Pará and Amazonas. Their language is part of the Tupi family.

[19] TR. The Sateré Mawé people are a group of approximately 13,000 people who live in the Brazilian Amazon, primarily in the state of Amazonas. Their language is part of the Tupi family.

the body of a river is irreplaceable. The city of São Paulo recklessly covered up its waterways, including the Ipiranga River,[20] on the banks of which Brazilian independence was proclaimed, suggesting that there exists not even the slightest appreciation for this memory. The rivers that haven't yet been suffocated by the cities continue to flow in the Cerrado,[21] in the forests, in the Atlantic Forest, and in the Pantanal – all plagued biomes. And these rivers are the first to have their bodies expropriated by the fury of certain humans in their incessant activities: these people who pollute the planet see rivers only as potential energy for the construction of dams or as volume for agriculture; and thus, Brazil continues to export its water through grains and minerals. People treat the rivers so disrespectfully that it seems as if they've suffered an affective collapse with regard to the precious gifts that life provides us here on Earth. Another appalling practice is the turning of riverbanks into pastures. After fifty years of seeing cattle, people, and machines trampling

---

[20] *TR.* The Ipiranga River is a creek that flows through the city of São Paulo, Brazil. It is historically known as the site where Dom Pedro I declared Brazil's independence from Portugal on September 7, 1822.

[21] *TR.* Understood as the biologically richest savanna in the world, the Cerrado is a tropical ecoregion making up a vast portion of eastern Brazil. Various groups, from Indigenous communities to *quilombola* communities to extractivists inhabit the Cerrado and live off the land.

the soil, rivers get tired. Yes, because when the landscape becomes unbearable, rivers migrate and flow into other pathways.

Rivers of memory, flying rivers, rivers that dive, sweat, and make rain.

During the eighteenth, nineteenth, and twentieth centuries, the São Francisco River served as a guide for millions of people; the river crosses several states, starting in Minas Gerais and flowing to the coast of Alagoas. As for the Doce River, our beloved Watu, it flows toward Espírito Santo. The two rivers take different paths: while one runs northeast, the other goes to the eastern region of Brazil, but both have arrived in the twenty-first century fractured, fragmented, dammed, and bleeding. Today, the body of Watu is filled with mercury and a long list of poisons from mining. It got tired and sank inside itself. The material that flows in its channel is no longer a river, but debris from an abusive civilization, which the great Chief Seattle referred to as vomit.[22] The true water, born in the mountains, now runs beneath a stone slab identified by

---

[22] *TR*. Chief Seattle, also known as Sealth or Si'ahl, was a prominent leader of the Suquamish and Duwamish people in the Pacific northwest region of the United States during the mid-nineteenth century. He was born in 1786 near Blake Island in what is now the state of Washington and lived until he was about 80 years old. The precise moment at which Chief Seattle referred to the debris as "vomit" remains unclear.

geologists as a formation of granite and other solid materials. On top of this platform, there are three layers of soil: the river has dived deep. It continues its journey toward the Atlantic Ocean, but no longer wants to expose itself to the constant abuse of this absurd idea that bodies exist to be exploited. It refuses to suffer this kind of bullying and, in the face of such offense, it disappears. Then people complain that they are running out of water, that they can no longer promote development and progress because humans, with their foolish economies, require unlimited amounts of water for hydroelectric power plants, factories, industries, cattle ranching, and agribusiness – and they're always complaining.

Living rivers.

Are we going to kill all the rivers? Will we turn all these marvelous, resilient beings capable of sculpting stones into a threat to life, causing them to disappear? In the early 1990s, a coalition called "Living Rivers" was created in the Amazon region to mobilize communities that opposed the construction of dams and waterways, to discuss river diversion projects and commercial navigation adaptation, to question all of this. Glenn Switkes[23] is a guy who was born in the

[23] TR. Glenn Switkes is an environmental activist who has worked on issues related to the Amazon rainforest for many

United States and whom I met in the 1980s when he came to Brazil to make a film about the Amazon. He ended up dedicating the next twenty or thirty years to getting to know our rivers and to strengthen an international campaign to keep them alive. People say that the amount of water that exists in the biosphere of planet Earth is the same as it was billions of years ago when the terrestrial ecosystems that we enjoy were formed. Faced with this argument, someone might ask: "Well, if water never diminishes, what's the problem?" The thing is, when we turn water into sewage, it goes into a coma, and it can take a long time for it to come alive again. What we're doing by polluting the waters that have existed for two billion years is putting an end to our own existence. Water will continue to exist here in the biosphere and slowly regenerate because rivers have that gift. It's we who have such an ephemeral existence that we'll end up dried up, as enemies of the water, even though we've learned that 70 percent of our bodies are made of water. If I were to dehydrate completely, all that would remain is half a kilo of bones, which is why I say: respect the water and learn its language. Let us

---

years. In the 1980s, he produced a documentary film called *Amazonia: Voices From the Rainforest*, which was released in 1991.

listen to the voices of the rivers, for they speak. Let us be like water in matter and spirit, in our movement and capacity to change courses, or we will be lost.

Cartographies for After the End

Going back, we could say that, in the beginning, there was the leaf. Other narratives will say that, in the beginning, there was the word. Yet others will create very different landscapes, and that is wonderful. Among so many worlds, I feel particularly touched by the stories that bring us closer to the beings invisible to the clouded eyes of those who cannot walk on Earth with the joy we should imprint in every gesture, in every breath. Indigenous ancestors said that when we placed a mast on the ground to perform our rituals, it marked the center of the world. It's magical that the center can be in so many places, but which world are we talking about? Because when we say "world," we usually think of this one, a "world" in constant dispute triggered by a management that has metastasized: capitalism, which some already call "the Capitalocene."

The challenge I propose here is to imagine cartographies, layers of worlds, in which the narratives are so diverse that we don't have to come to blows when evoking different creation stories. It's wonderful that these memories still exist in the traditions of hundreds of peoples, whether in the Americas, Africa, Asia... These narratives are gifts that are continuously offered to us, and it's so beautiful that they give meaning to the unique experiences of each group of people in different contexts experiencing life on this planet. For some time, despite always thinking from where I am – by the side of this river – when I extend my gaze to other places on Earth, the dreamt cartographies I see include that fantastic image of an astronaut who, looking down from space, exclaimed: "The Earth is blue!" The planet is indeed marvelous and it is embraced, in various Indigenous traditions – from Tierra del Fuego to Alaska – by a poetics permeated with maternal significance.

Our Guarani relatives from the Atlantic Forest,[24] from this seaside border they call *"nhé ere,"* or the place that produces life, perceive the region as both a landscape and an incessant source of life. The first time these dear relatives shared their

[24] *TR.* The Guarani people from the Atlantic coast of Brazil live primarily in the southern and southeastern regions of the country, particularly in the states of São Paulo, Paraná, Santa Catarina, and Rio Grande do Sul.

narrative of world creation with me, I learned that two primordial twins had to bend the Serra do Mar[25] and create that foothill so that the Big Water, the sea, would not flow onto the continent. I found this story beautiful, as it explains the topography – the formation of mountains, valleys, and bodies of water they inhabit. The fact is that the Guarani, like the *caiçaras*[26] of the region, are squeezed into small plots, reduced to islands from which they bravely resist real estate speculation, the occupation of their territories, and the violence that devastates this place their spirits see, and their words translate, through an affective cartography.

The Tikmu'un,[27] also known as Maxakali, who are here in the Vale do Mucuri, neighbors of the Doce River, speak beautifully about this land from which they were dispossessed. Unlike other peoples

[25] TR. Serra do Mar is a mountain range that is located along the southeastern coast of Brazil, running parallel to the Atlantic Ocean. It covers large parts of the states of Rio Grande do Sul, Santa Catarina, Paraná, São Paulo, and Rio de Janeiro.
[26] TR. *Caiçara* is a term used in Brazil to describe a traditional way of life that is practiced in coastal regions of the country, particularly in the southeastern states of São Paulo, Paraná, and Santa Catarina. *Caiçara* communities are typically small fishing villages or settlements.
[27] TR. The Tikmu'un people, also known as the Maxakali, are an Indigenous group that lives in the eastern region of Brazil, primarily in the states of Minas Gerais and Bahia. They speak a language that is part of the Macro-Jê family.

native to this area, who had one or another reser-
vation established by the government, the Maxakali
spent the seventeenth, eighteenth, and nineteenth
centuries without a place to rest their heads. But
now they've decided to occupy an ancient territory
their narratives talk about, and these folks are
capable of restoring the entire fauna and flora of
that place where there are almost no more animals
and plants. Amidst the desert of pastures that the
region has become during the twentieth century, the
Maxakali can see the forest and evoke the names of
all the insects, reptiles, birds, venomous animals,
plants, and fungi that existed there, pointing out
each one's place in the landscape. Any scholar
would be amazed by this inventory and by their
ability to restore the presence of beings that have
already become extinct in this land: the Maxakali
are there, representing this whole gradient of life.
In the midst of a farming culture, they can see a
territory full of spirits and speak with the invisible
world. A people like this, even when dispossessed
of everything and without even having ground to
stand on, can still recreate a place to inhabit.

When I think about the movement of the Watu, I
perceive its power: a body of water on the surface
that had the capacity to dive into the Earth in
search of deep aquifers and to reshape its path
when under attack. Thus, it teaches us to avoid
further damage. In this so-called Capitalocene that

we're experiencing, there won't be any place on Earth left untouched, just like the body of this river, devastated by mud. Mud will reach every corner of the planet, just as polymers and microplastics can reach the belly of every fish in the ocean. Why must these animals carry these substances within their light and beautiful bone structures? An expert in the field told me that microplastics travel through our bodies and can already be found in newborn babies. I found this scandalous, but we cannot surrender to the doomsday narrative that haunts us because it serves to make us give up on our dreams, and within our dreams lie the memories of the Earth and our ancestors.

We are living in a world in which we are forced to delve deep into the Earth to be able to recreate possible worlds. However, in narratives where only humans act, this centrality silences all other presences. They make attempts to silence the *encantados* [enchanted ones],[28] reducing

---

[28] TR. The term "*encantados*" is a concept that is often used in Indigenous contexts in Brazil. In various Indigenous cultures, the *encantados* are seen as guardians of the environment and are revered and respected by many people. Many Indigenous communities have stories and traditions passed down over generations about the *encantados*, and they are often featured in ceremonies and rituals. Some Indigenous communities also believe that humans can be transformed into *encantados* after death, and that they may continue to play an important role in the world of the living.

this "spiritual life" to mimicry, suppressing the experience of bodies in communion with leaves, lichen, water, wind, fire, with everything that activates our transcendent power and surpasses the mediocrity to which humans have reduced themselves. This is offensive to me. Humans are accepting the humiliating condition of consuming the Earth. The Orishas, as well as the Indigenous ancestors and those of other traditions, created worlds where we could experience life and sing and dance, but it seems that the will of capital is to impoverish existence. Capitalism wants a grim and monotonous world where we operate like robots. We cannot accept that.

There is a poet from the Kuna[29] people in Panama named Cebaldo Inawinapi. He is currently a professor at a university in Porto, Portugal, but he frequently visits the island of Kunayala,[30] where his people live. He tells a story about how the birth of a Kuna child involves identifying the body that arrives with a tree. Just like the Krenak people, they relate the child's umbilical cord to a

---

[29] *TR*. The Kuna people, also known as the Guna, are an Indigenous group primarily residing in the coastal regions of Panama and Colombia. The Kuna language, known as Dulegaya, is part of the Chibchan language family.

[30] *TR*. The forests of Kunayala, also known as the Kuna Yala or Guna Yala, are located in northeastern Panama along the Caribbean coast.

plant. Inawinapi says that all the Kunayala forests are formed by people; they have names, because each plant coincides with someone who was born there. This movement between a human body and a plant can occur with a banana tree or with a tree that lives for two hundred years – it doesn't matter. What's important is burying the umbilical cord when doing the planting so that the child and the plant share the same spirit. When João Paulo Barreto speaks about the conception of the body made of clay in the tradition of the Tukano people from the upper Negro River, he's also saying that there is no boundary between the human body and other organisms around it. A long time ago, we convinced ourselves that we are this excellent thing called "humans" and we refrained from expanding into other organisms beyond this sanitary and hygienic human figure. This configuration of the body that many accept today is merely a poor institution manufactured by a civilization without imagination.

When I talk about postponing the end of the world, I'm not referring to the collapse of this world. I wish this violent world would disappear at midnight tonight, and that tomorrow we wake up in a new one. However, in reality, we are acting on the prospect of transfiguration, desiring what Nêgo Bispo calls *confluences*, and not that exorbitant euphoria of monoculture that gathers the crazies who celebrate necropolitics rather than the plural life of the peoples on this planet. Unlike what they are doing, *confluences* evoke the context of diverse worlds that can affect each other. It is a term carved by the local craftsmanship of a *quilombola*[31] man, a brilliant marginal thinker in this colonial universe, a calm and humorous critic of political trends.

In turn, political *convergence* has been an issue in South America for the last forty or fifty years. It embraces ideas such as the possibility that Argentine Peronism would fuse into modern politics, or that Brazil could combine a kind of laborism with capitalism in order to produce a new experience of neoliberal political governance that would replace colonialism... But Nêgo Bispo escapes this grammar by saying that he is interested in confluences, and, at the same time, he is able to produce an analysis that links these confluences to both convergences and divergences. Without denying political events or attempting to escape the historical sense of things, he says that we don't need to be subordinate to this same logic and instead tries to develop a perspective in which confluences do not encompass everything but open possibilities for other worlds.

---

[31] *TR.* "Quilombola" is a term used in Brazil to describe the descendants of enslaved African peoples who fled from captivity and established independent maroon communities, known as *quilombos*.

These openings even allow us to refuse to be complicit with the colonial discourse as if it were our last chance for reconciliation: "Oh, in order for us to understand ourselves as a nation, let's all pretend there was no genocide." How can we consider a homeland's history in the midst of this continental cemetery? We have to rebel, and confluences can help us with that. If colonialism has brought upon us a nearly irreparable harm, it is precisely the harm of claiming that we are all the same. Now we'll have to refute that and evoke the worlds of affective cartographies, in which the river can escape harm, life can escape stray bullets, and freedom is not just the condition of accepting the subject, but such a radical experience that it takes us beyond the idea of finitude. We're not going to stop dying or anything like that; rather, we will transfigure ourselves because metamorphosis is our environment, similar to the leaves, branches, and everything that exists.

Cities, Pandemics, and Other Gadgets

The experience of the COVID-19 pandemic was devastating. On one occasion, when I was asked to comment on this turn of events, someone asked me: "Ailton, did COVID teach us anything?" I replied: "Why do you think it should teach us something? Pandemics don't happen in order to teach us something, but to devastate our lives. If you think that someone who comes to kill you is going to teach you something, it's only to teach you to run or hide." I'm sorry if I'm being offensive to white people, but I don't know where this mentality – that suffering teaches something – comes from. If it did, the diasporic peoples, who went through the unutterable tragedy of slavery, would be rewarded in the twenty-first century. I don't buy into this idea; I don't want to learn anything at the cost of suffering.

I also believe that our psychological accommo-
dation to the virtual environment, which intensified
during this period, cannot be healthy. When the
pandemic started, I warned people, saying things
like: "Remember, this is virtual, it's a screen, we
are not directly talking to each other," because I
believe that, between our actions in this virtual
environment and their results, a gap can be created
by a misunderstanding and even confusion. I have
noticed that I am exposing myself too much,
abusing the technology, and observing that it can
foster the illusion that we are obtaining results
or success. You dedicate hours on end to this
environment and think you are moving something,
but, in reality, we can stay there for a lifetime
without moving anything.

In the not-so-distant future, we will all be transformed into spectators. We won't need to do
anything anymore: people will connect as soon
as they wake up, just like workers punching in,
and then disconnect when it's time to go to sleep.
And we'll be able to consume everything we want
throughout our lives because capitalism will provide
everything for us! Professor Conceição Evaristo[32]
said something brilliant: people find it easier to

[32] *TR.* Conceição Evaristo (b. 1946) is known for her
literary works that explore themes of race, gender, and social
inequality, focusing on the experiences of Black women in
Brazil. Evaristo's works include the novel *Ponciá Vicêncio*

end the world than to end capitalism.[33] It's true, we have simply become complacent about the idea that capitalism will never end; on the contrary, it will clog us up with more and more stuff, and we'll have so much food, so much drink, so much of everything that nothing will be lacking. And so we keep going, cloistered in the metropolis, allowing this absurd idea to guide us.

Historically, the city has been opposed to what we call "the forest" to the point that childhood imagination fixates on Little Red Riding Hood and is threatened by a wolf or a werewolf, a plague, any creature that will jump out of the forest to devour us. In fact, one of the narratives about COVID-19 suggests that it started because there was a forest:

> Some guys who used to go to a market in Wuhan went into the woods to gather firewood. They found an owl, stepped on its tail, captured a wild pangolin, called it ugly, and brought it to live with tamed animals at the market. Then the virus that was in the wild animal passed to the healthy animals, who then

---

(2003), the short story collection *Insubmissas lágrimas de mulheres* (2011), and the novel *Becos da memória* (2016).

[33] TR. A similar notion is often attributed to Fredric Jameson and Slavoj Žižek. For more on how capitalism has come to dominate our imaginations and limit our ability to envision alternative socioeconomic systems, see *Capitalist Realism: Is There No Alternative?* by Mark Fisher, who also references this idea.

passed it on to us, and it spread across the planet as part of a Chinese tactical move.

This narrative is very malicious but it has had a significant impact.

These seemingly random comments I'm making about the pandemic, the origin of the virus, and the hole in the city wall are topics I've been reflecting on intensely during this period because I, too, was trapped. I diligently followed the recommendations of the World Health Organization: I tried to avoid infection, took the vaccines, and didn't leave my village. And I began to reevaluate the normalization of getting into a car and going wherever, boarding a plane and going to the other side of the world. Because just as we can normalize life on a screen and immerse ourselves in virtual experience, since the end of the twentieth century, we've also normalized the use of a bunch of machines as if they were extensions of our bodies. Eduardo Viveiros de Castro[34] has a text called *Fatherland Involunteers*, and here I would like to suggest an expansion of that statement, and say that we are all becoming involuntary participants in a world

---

[34] *TR*. Eduardo Viveiros de Castro (b. 1951) is a Brazilian ethnologist known for his influential contributions to anthropological theory, particularly within the field of Indigenous studies. Viveiros de Castro's work revolves around Indigenous cosmologies, social organization, and epistemologies.

that has normalized a thousand gadgets as our extensions. Thus, progress rules over us, and we continue on autopilot, furiously devouring the planet.

The city has become the black box of civilization. The Earth's body can't bear cities anymore, at least not those that resemble a continuation of the ancient *polis*, with people protected by walls and the rest left outside – whether it's wild animals or Indigenous peoples, *quilombolas*, riverine peoples, or people from rural areas. Moreover, metropolises are energy sinkholes. There are still those who have the audacity to say that Brazil is a pioneer in clean energy production. I don't know what that is all about; if you were to put a blood filter on the hydroelectric plants of Tucuruí, Balbina, Belo Monte, Santo Antônio, and Jirau, it would clog.

José Mujica, the former president of Uruguay, says that we are replacing the idea of citizenship with the consumer experience, and thus the world becomes inhabited by customers – some of whom are preferred ones. To make things even more of a zoo, there are many people who want to live forever: people who are afraid of dying. The butterfly dies; the bird comes flying, hits its head here and dies; the bee reproduces and dies; the banana tree grows, bears fruit, and dies... We are the only damn beings on the planet who want to prevail at all costs and, of course, not be added to the endangered species list. There's an interesting quote attributed to Einstein: "Life started here on Earth without humans, and it can end without us." That "can" is his caution against completely detonating the bomb. As for me, I'm more arrogant and say that life began without humans and will end without us. We don't hold the keys, nor will we be the last to leave. In fact, I think we will be expelled – due to incompetence, noncompliance, abuse, and all kinds of misdemeanors we have engaged in to prolong our own lives.

The city itself is an attempt to do this *ad aeternum*. Maybe that's why Rome was called "the eternal city." That title sounds beautiful, but what does it conceal? Isn't this precisely the persistent desire of humans to perpetuate themselves on the planet? Rome was a very long-lasting empire and established a significant part of the elements that constitute our urban repertoire, which was calibrated during this long period of human arrogance. The Romans themselves decided to rule the world by decree, based on the will of a guy named Caesar, who was given full power: he killed, beheaded, burned, plundered everything, and then sorted things out with God, who was his boss. I don't know which God that was. The fundamental issue is that we started to imitate this model and constructed cities that spread all over the world.

Urbanization in Brazil began late. Even in the 1960s and 1970s, there were campaigns for people to leave the countryside and move to urban centers, which resulted in a massive exodus from rural regions. Many people left rural areas to make way for agribusiness and ended up starving in the cities. According to Viveiros de Castro as well, Brazil has specialized in producing poor people. Our technology for producing poverty goes more or less like this: we take those who fish and gather native fruits, remove them from their territory, and dump them into the outskirts of the city, where they will never again be able to catch a fish to eat because the river flowing through the neighborhood is so polluted. If you take a Yanomami person out of the forest, where they have water, food, and autonomy, and put them in Boa Vista, that's the production of poverty. If you forcibly displace people from the Volta Grande do Xingu[35] to build a hydroelectric plant, sending

---

[35] *TR*. Volta Grande do Xingu is a region located in the state of Pará, in the northern region of Brazil. It's a section of the Xingu River that is approximately 100 kilometers long, spanning the municipalities of Altamira and Vitória do Xingu. It is an ecologically rich area, home to diverse species of flora and fauna, including several endangered species. The region is also home to several Indigenous communities, including the Juruna, Arara, and Xikrin people, who rely

them to the outskirts of Altamira, you are making them poor.

Capitalism needs a platform – an urban one. Just look at cities like New York and Tokyo, where the stock exchanges are – they're the anchors of this system. Moreover, urbanity establishes a way of life that is already being called necrocapitalism, but the ontology of the subject born in the city, who develops an urban way of thinking, is so powerful that they end up influencing other cultures worldwide. Thus, through the gestures and collaboration of each individual – from the newborn who is already a consumer to the elderly who die hooked up to some technological apparatus because they don't have the courage to die at home – the urban sphere establishes itself as the only possible destination for humans.

The image I have of cities has something to do with Superman fighting against Lex Luthor, where, because of kryptonite, the more he struggles, the stronger the villain becomes. The way I see it,

---

on the river and surrounding forests for their livelihoods. In recent years, the Belo Monte hydroelectric dam, which became operational in 2016, caused significant environmental and social impacts in the region, including the displacement of Indigenous communities and the disruption of fishing practices.

a city is Mariana,[36] Ouro Preto,[37] even Dubai. I think of Itanhaém, with that fort, which is a Jesuit convent,[38] where people would gather to pray and also to shoot because there were cannons on top of those high walls. So, the city is an apparatus capable of promoting religion and a certain way of thinking, but it's also armed to expand its dominion. If we were to blame someone for the current state of cities, who would we point the cannons of Itanhaém at? Engineers, architects, and urban planners? Developers, real estate speculators, and construction companies? City council members

[36] *TR.* Mariana is a historic town located in the state of Minas Gerais, Brazil. It is located approximately 120 kilometers south of the state capital, Belo Horizonte. In November 2015, a catastrophic dam failure occurred near Mariana. The dam, which was owned and operated by the mining company Samarco, released millions of cubic meters of toxic waste and other debris into the surrounding waterways, houses, and forests. The disaster is considered one of the worst environmental catastrophes in Brazilian history. It claimed the lives of nineteen people.

[37] *TR.* Ouro Preto is a historic town located in the state of Minas Gerais, Brazil. It is a UNESCO World Heritage site and is known for its Baroque architecture and cultural heritage. The town was founded in the late seventeenth century during Brazil's colonial period, and was an important center of gold mining and trade.

[38] *TR.* A reference to the Convent Nossa Senhora da Conceição, which was founded by the Jesuits in the sixteenth century during the period of Portuguese colonization. The convent is located in the city of Itanhaém, in the state of São Paulo, Brazil.

with their amendments and repairs? What determines the character of a city?

Modern architecture has elaborated on the maxim that civilization needs cement and iron. This thought relates to the world in terms of the consumption of nonrenewable resources: if you use iron, one day it'll run out; if you use cement, one day it'll run out. If you do a project that needs cement, stone, iron, glass, and the rest, it's the same as using fossil fuel. I don't know of any mountain that will produce cement and stone again after they've been extracted from its body. If we devour the mountains and swallow the Earth's subsoil to build cities, what we're doing, as Drummond[39] would say, is mobilizing the world's machinery.

But let's not only look at the European part of this story; let's not lose sight of the cities that Africa, China, and India have constructed. How do Asian cultures see cities? Do they see them in the same way as Western cultures? I have the impression that they use a different vocabulary when talking about cities. In fact, Westerners often complain about the promiscuity of Indian urbanity, with animals

[39] TR. Carlos Drummond de Andrade was a Brazilian poet and writer who lived from 1902 to 1987. Drummond was one of the key figures of Brazilian modernism, and is known for his striking imagery, innovative use of language, and social commentary.

mixed with people in the streets and in the Ganges River, and they deride Indian people as if there were only one way to live – the Western model. These epistemes, which are produced from a specific position of conceptualizing the world, dictate the idea of what is dirty versus what is clean.

The sanitary culture that supposedly regulates everything operates under the following logic: to sanitize is to urbanize, and to urbanize is to sanitize. This makes me think of a group of young medical professionals in the health sciences who produced some interesting work about the pandemic; they stated that this event strengthens authoritarianism, granting governments even more control over our lives. This made me imagine that the entire planet will become a kind of general hospital, and, instead of hunting terrorists, the police will pursue those who are not properly sanitized. They'll do inspections of people's nails, and if they're dirty, they'll kill them. We'll end up with a dystopia where that which isn't a city isn't sanitized, isn't properly clean, will be eliminated from the map.

In this way, the forest, woods, and living ecosystems, with their obvious capacity to produce life and also viruses, will be surrounded to prevent those ecosystems from contaminating the cities. So, it goes like this: walls built to protect some humans end up confining forests. Does what I'm saying sound absurd? Well, I had a vision of this back in 1993 when Davi Kopenawa,[40] Cipassé Xavante,[41] and I were taken to Milan after the Eco-92 conference – when Brazil seemed like the most interesting place in the world for those thinking about ecology in Europe. On that occasion, a very wealthy lady, heiress to some transportation companies, hired an advisor and said: "Find interesting Indigenous people in Latin America and the United States, bring a bunch of them together, and bring them to me." In addition to the three of us, there was an Oglala Lakota elder from the United States, and a shaman from the Kogi people from the Sierra Nevada in Colombia.

[40] *TR.* Davi Kopenawa (b. 1956) is a Yanomami Indigenous leader and shaman who advocates for Indigenous peoples, and specifically the Yanomami, and the protection of the Amazon rainforest. He plays a significant role in raising awareness about the struggles faced by Indigenous communities in Brazil. He has been involved in various social and political movements aimed at promoting Indigenous rights and cultural preservation, including the Hutukara Yanomami Association, which he founded in the 1980s. Through his collaboration with anthropologist Bruce Albert, Kopenawa coauthored *The Falling Sky: Words of a Yanomami Shaman*, which was published in English in 2013.

[41] *TR.* Paulo Cipassé Xavante is a Xavante leader from the Wederá village, which is located in the Pimentel Barbosa Indigenous Land in the state of Mato Grosso, in central-western Brazil. The Xavante are one of the largest Indigenous groups in the country. Their language belongs to the Jê family.

This lady had a palace with a greenhouse, like the ones used to keep snakes at the Butantã Institute.[42] Inside this garden, there was a tree. I looked at that sad tree, which was the size of a jabuticabeira, and the people in the house couldn't even tell me what it was. So I asked: "Did you make a monument to this unknown tree?" I think we are heading into a sinkhole as absurd as that of those Italian millionaires' palaces, and we're dealing with these tree-beings that existed long before us with such blatant disrespect and abuse that we will end up destroying the planet's last forests without even realizing it or knowing their names.

Here's an essential issue that's been bothering me: "How could the idea that life is wild impact the production of urbanistic thinking today?" It's a call for an epistemological rebellion, to collaborate with the production of life. When I say that life is wild, I want to draw attention to an existential potency, which has a forgotten poetics, abandoned by the schools that educate the professionals who perpetuate the logic that civilization is urban, and

---

[42] *TR*. The Butantã Institute is a biomedical research center located in the city of São Paulo, Brazil. It was founded in 1901 and is one of the oldest and most prestigious research institutions in Latin America. It specializes in the production of immunobiologicals, vaccines, antivenoms, and other products derived from biological materials, in particular for snake bites, spider bites, and other types of venomous bites and stings.

everything outside cities is barbaric, primitive – and that people can set it on fire.

How do we scale the walls of cities? What are the possible implications of human communities living in the forest versus those closed off in the metropolis? If we can ensure that forests continue to exist in the world, there will be communities within them. I saw a figure published in a report by the World Wide Fund for Nature (WWF) stating that 1.4 billion people in the world depend on the forest, meaning there's an economy linked to it. These are not the lumber industry folks; it's an economy that assumes humans living there need the forest to survive.

Anthropologist Lux Vidal wrote a very important work on Indigenous habitats, which connects materials and concepts that organize the idea of a balanced habitat in harmony with their surroundings: the land, the sun, the moon, the stars – a habitat integrated into the cosmos, which is different from the prosthesis that cities have become worldwide. So, I wonder, how can we make the forest exist within us, within our homes, within our yards? We can spark the emergence of *florestania*[43] by contesting this sanitary urban order,

[43] TR. *Florestania*, as understood by Ailton Krenak and as described in the Introduction, is a constant struggle to expand the space for exercising citizenship beyond urban settings. In cities, the idea of citizenship is often tied to paved

by saying: I will let my yard grow wild; I want to study its grammar. How do I find a trumpet tree, a red peroba, or a jacaranda in the middle of the woods? What if I had a moriche palm tree in my yard?

We need to stop this compulsion to cover everything with asphalt and cement. Our streams are suffocating because of a catacomb mentality, exacerbated by sanitary policies, that assumes that a concrete slab should be placed on any small stream, as if having running water there were discreditable. The sinuosity of riverbeds is unbearable for the straight, concrete, upright minds of those

---

streets, portable water, sanitation, real estate, privatized property, public services, security, police, healthcare, and hospitals. Conversely, *florestania* shows that citizenship is not solely an urban prerogative. It has to do with the ability to organize and advocate for the forest, biodiversity, and life at large within contexts that aren't necessarily urban. In the late 1980s and early 1990s, the term *florestania* began to gain wider recognition after being coined by Antonio Alves Leitao Neto, an advisor to the state government in Acre in northern Brazil. In that context, the notion of *florestania* sought to reverse the implied emphasis on *cidade* (city) within the concept of *cidadania* (citizenship), highlighting the intention of extending citizenship to previously excluded residents of the forests. This term captures the goals, rights, and obligations associated with promoting development rooted in the defense of the forest environment. See Marianne Schmink, "Forest citizens: Changing life conditions and social identities in the land of the rubber tappers," *Latin American Research Review* 46.S1 (2011): 141–158.

who work in urban planning. Most of the time nowadays, urban planning is executed against the landscape. How can we convert industrial urban fabric into natural urban fabric, centering nature and transforming cities from within?

I was invited to participate in one of Bia Lessa's projects,[44] which utilizes virtual reality technologies. She went to the Largo do Paissandu[45] area to look at the building, which had been occupied by homeless people, that caught fire.[46] (By the way, only a city can produce such a gruesome event, with a bunch of people inside a burning building.) Bia became interested in those ruins and intensified the dystopia by putting zombies inside and making things even more absurd; she then went in and transformed it in collaboration with many professionals in architecture, engineering, urban planning, recycling, environmentalism, and ecology. She referenced Glauber Rocha and the characters from *Earth*

[44] *TR.* Bia Lessa is a prominent Brazilian theater director, set designer, and cultural producer. She is known for her innovative and experimental approach to theater.

[45] *TR.* Largo do Paissandu is a historic square located in the center of São Paulo.

[46] *TR.* A reference to the fire at Edifício Wilton Paes de Almeida in Largo do Paissandu, São Paulo, which occurred on May 1, 2018. The building, which was occupied by homeless families, caught fire, collapsed, and resulted in several casualties, highlighting concerns about housing safety and urban inequality.

Entranced in the scene and created a utopia within those ruins.[47] I proposed uncovering the streams. So, using virtual reality, we ripped up the floor of Paissandu (that *bandeirante*[48] site in downtown São Paulo, which is very symbolic) and turned the stream that flows through there into a waterfall. We simulated the emergence of vegetation and animals in the square. We summoned Hélio Oiticica,[49]

[47] *TR.* Brazilian filmmaker Glauber Rocha (1939–81) was a key figure in the Cinema Novo movement, which sought to challenge the dominant narratives of Brazilian cinema and create a new kind of national cinema that reflected the realities of Brazilian life and culture. Some of his most famous films include *Black God, White Devil* (1964) and *Earth Entranced* (1967).

[48] *TR. Bandeirante* is a term used to describe a group of explorers who played a significant role in the colonization of Brazil. The *bandeirantes* were mostly of mixed-race or white Portuguese descent and originated from São Paulo and other parts of Brazil's southeast region. They were known for their expeditions, or *bandeiras*, into the interior of Brazil in the seventeenth and eighteenth centuries. These expeditions were organized with the goal of capturing Indigenous people for slave labor and/or discovering precious metals and gems.

[49] *TR.* Hélio Oiticica (b. 1937) is a Brazilian artist. He is considered one of the most important figures in Brazilian and Latin American art and is known for his radical approach to artistic practice. Oiticica's work combined elements of painting, sculpture, installation art, and performance to create immersive environments that blur the boundaries between art and life. Two of his most famous series are called "*Parangolé*," which consists of wearable textile structures that were intended to be worn and used as part of a performance, and "Penetrables," which were immersive and

with his *"parangolés"* and "penetrables," and we
tore down the walls of the buildings. The iron and
concrete skeletons were hollowed out, and wind,
rain, sun, and forestry passed through the physical
matter of the city – because life demands such
enjoyment.

When Marilena Chauí[50] was the Secretary of
Culture of São Paulo, she organized a discussion
about the public and the private in urban space.
On that occasion, it became very clear that the
modern city does not tolerate the commons;[51] on
the contrary, it is hostile to it. There was a lot of

---

participatory artworks designed to be entered and experienced by viewers, allowing them to physically engage with
the space and materials.

[50] *TR.* Marilena Chauí (b. 1941) is a Brazilian philosopher,
educator, and political activist and has become one of the
most important and influential figures in Brazilian intellectual
life in recent decades. Her work focuses on a wide range of
topics, including political philosophy, critical theory, and
education. She has written extensively on the history of
philosophy, and has been a leading voice in the development
of critical theory in Brazil.

[51] *TR.* "O comum," rendered here as "the commons,"
conjures a sense of that which is shared or common among
peoples, be it culture, space, or forms of life. While the
English phrasing "the commons" appears to allude to an
array of meanings endemic to the history of critical theory,
Krenak is not directly citing or referring to a particular usage.
On the contrary, his notion of "*o comum*" at once shares and
exceeds the uses of the concept in Western critical theory and
philosophy.

discussion about what should be public, about the space where people could move around. But, increasingly, an ATM would pop up and get in the way. The discussion was about the extent to which public space could be occupied while the municipality had a license to impose fees and charge for each use. What kind of "common" keeps getting invaded by people who can appropriate it?

The thing is, "the commons" is not an abstraction; it is made up of bodies that walk, breathe, eat, and imagine. And if these bodies have no place in cities, then cities are no place for the commons. Father Julio Lancellotti[52] took a sledgehammer to knock down spikes placed under a viaduct in São Paulo to prevent people from lying down. Cities may have been the home of the commons in their pre-industrial beginnings, for a brief moment. Today, however, cities act against it like machines. Perhaps that building occupied by the homeless in the Paissandu area was an experience of the commons within the city, but nobody wanted it there, and it was treated as an inconvenience. So it

---

[52] *TR.* Father Julio Lancellotti is a Brazilian Catholic priest who has dedicated his life to social work and activism. He is known for his advocacy work in helping Brazil's poor and marginalized communities, particularly homeless individuals and people living with HIV/AIDS. Father Lancellotti has worked for several decades in the city of São Paulo, where he has helped to establish soup kitchens, health clinics, and other social services for people living in poverty.

caught fire and, after the fire, nobody went to fix it – as if the commons should be moved elsewhere.

Cities have been invaded by industry and production, transforming the logic of collective life into private life. It is valuable to observe that the records about the Mayas and the Aztecs speak of very urban cultures, but in an expanded sense. They do not specifically evoke cities, but a way of being and belonging to a collective dynamic. In this sense, the peoples who live in the Xingu territory are also quite urban with their garden-cities. When Davi Kopenawa narrates the alliances between humans and the *xapiri*,[53] the spirits of the forest, he is referring to the same thing. We need to reforest our imagination, and thus, perhaps, we can reconnect with a poetics of urbanity that restores the power of life instead of constantly repeating what the Greeks and Romans did. Let's build a forest, hanging gardens amid urban life, where there can be a little more desire, joy, life, and pleasure, rather than tiles covering streams and rivers. After all, life is wild and also blossoms in cities.

[53] TR. The *xapiri* are central entities in Yanomami cosmology. They communicate with shamans through visions and dreams, and play an important role in healing rituals and other types of spiritual practices. They are also often depicted in Yanomami art, particularly in the form of drawings.

Affective Alliances

The word "citizenship" is well known: it appears in the Universal Declaration of Human Rights and in various constitutions. It is part of – let's call it – the white repertoire. The notion of *florestania*, on the other hand, originated in a regional context, at a very dynamic moment in the social struggles of the peoples who live in the forest. When Chico Mendes,[54] rubber tree tappers, and Indigenous

[54] *TR*. Chico Mendes, whose full name was Francisco Alves Mendes Filho, was a Brazilian rubber tree tapper, trade union leader, and environmental activist. He dedicated his life to fighting for the rights of rubber tree tappers and the preservation of the Amazon rainforest. He played a key role in organizing and advocating for sustainable extraction practices that would protect both the livelihoods of local communities and the environment. He was born on December 15, 1944, in Xapuri, Acre, Brazil, and was assassinated on December 22, 1988.

peoples began to work together, they realized that what they wanted was not synonymous with citizenship. What they aspired to would be a new means for claiming rights. (After all, rights are not pre-existing things. They arise from a community's willingness to anticipate the understanding that something should be considered a right, but still isn't.) At the end of the 1970s, before the end of the dictatorship, the Brazilian government wanted to break up vast expanses of forest in the south of the Amazon and in Acre, close to the borders with Bolivia and Peru. The classic way of doing this was to build highways and bring settlers in; however, during an attempt to privatize that area in a discreet and efficient manner, the Incra people,[55] who were inspired by Jarbas Passarinho and his allies,[56] started offering allotments to the

---

[55] TR. Incra is the acronym for Brazil's National Institute of Colonization and Agrarian Reform (Instituto Nacional de Colonização e Reforma Agrária). It is a government agency charged with implementing and promoting agrarian reform policies throughout the country. Incra's primary objective is to ensure the social function of land by promoting redistribution, rural development, and the improvement of rural workers' living conditions.

[56] TR. Jarbas Passarinho was a Brazilian politician and military officer. Passarinho had a long political career in Brazil. During the military regime, he held several government positions. He was born on January 11, 1920, in Xapuri, Acre, Brazil, and passed away on June 5, 2016, in Brasília, Brazil.

people who were already there. It turns out that
when the state arrived to draw the settlement lines,
those who sided with Chico Mendes stood up (in
the spirit of *florestania*) and, like Gandhi and his
followers, organized a peaceful resistance to the
state's action. Women, children, men, and people of
all ages planted themselves among the trees and the
chainsaws, blocking the paths of those who arrived
to make the demarcations and preventing the urban
finger – whether of geographers, topographers, or
seismographers – from pinpointing the ends of the
forest. The people didn't want stakes or allotments;
they wanted the fluidity of the river, the continuity
of the forest.

The Indigenous people lived in collective
reserves, and the rubber tree tappers, who were
mostly northeastern Brazilians who migrated to
the Amazon at the end of the nineteenth century,
noticed this difference. After four, five, six generations in the forest, what they wanted was to live
like the Indigenous peoples. There was a fruitful
dissemination of ideas and culture, a reflection
about the commons, in which the rubber tree
tappers who created extractive reserves[57] equated
the status of these direct-use conservation units

---

[57] *TR.* Extractive reserves are protected areas of land that are
legally dedicated to local communities for natural resource
extraction – in this case, for rubber tapping.

with that of Indigenous lands. But we know that collective property does not exist in Brazil. Even the lands that Indigenous people inhabit belong to the state. The cancer of capitalism only recognizes private property and is incompatible with any other understanding of collective land use. In our aim to form *florestania*, we didn't even want to have a CPF.[58] But instituting a new law involves the mobilization of a massive apparatus made up of records, documents, certifications, notaries... What brought these people together was the understanding that among them there were people in power: landowners who claimed ownership of vast regions of the forest, the rubber plantations, where both Indigenous and non-Indigenous peoples were subjected to conditions of slave labor. A constellation of peoples such as the Kashinawa, the Ashaninka, the Huni Kuin, and many others were oppressed by this capitalist situation, in which a landowner who wasn't even there (he could be in São Paulo, London, or anywhere in the world) exploited the Amazon rainforest – and its people

[58] *TR.* CPF stands for "Cadastro de Pessoas Físicas," which translates to "Individual Taxpayer Registry." It is a unique identification number assigned to Brazilian citizens and foreign residents living in Brazil for various legal and financial purposes, and can serve a similar purpose to an American social security number, although CPFs are used more widely and frequently.

– by remote control. When we rose up to eliminate the figure of the landowner, it became possible for us to join together. The Forest Peoples Alliance (Aliança dos Povos da Floresta)[59] arose from the fight for equality in this political history.

It just so happens that the word politics comes from *polis*, and when human beings who are not from the *polis* think, they can imagine other worlds that are not political, or at least not like current politics. Language is very decisive in interactions, and everything that comes from the *polis* bears the mark of a gathering of equals, where political experiences are meant to converge. This inspired me to observe that the *polis* is always claimed as the world of culture, and that which is marked as nature is the wild world. And so I am interested in this other world, and not in the convergence that leads to the *polis*. I imagine powers converging through it, passing through it, but without getting trapped there. I think what the Zapatistas want is also *florestania*, but their act of claiming it was understood as a rebellion, and they were treated

---

[59] *ED.* Created in 1980, the Forest Peoples Alliance (Aliança dos Povos da Floresta) was born from a coalition of Indigenous leaders and rubber tree tappers in the Amazon. They demanded the demarcation of Indigenous territories and the creation of extractive reserves. Ailton Krenak was one of the founders of this movement, which peaked under the leadership of Chico Mendes, who was assassinated in 1988 for his activism.

as enemies and brutally suppressed. They ended up forced to wear the Zapatista mask and, in a way, to take on the limited space that the act of rebellion shaped. Everyone who is Zapatista has to live in the Lacandon Jungle, because Zapatismo only exists in Chiapas. They ended up trapped by their own insurgent thinking. *Florestania* cannot be a franchise; if we want to induce profound interrogation with the power of an insurrection, we cannot become prisoners of the movements we create. That's why, at a certain point, I began to ask myself how far we were going to go with the Forest Peoples Alliance: were we going to unionize, to become a political party? Political alliances, and even those alliances that acknowledge the existence of diversity, necessitate an equality that can become oppressive.

This experience of intense dedication lasted for more than twenty years, until I began to question the ongoing search for the proof of equality, and, for the first time, I became aware of the concept of affective alliances, which presupposes an affective bond between worlds that are not equal. This conception does not demand equality; on the contrary, it recognizes an intrinsic otherness in each person, in each being. It introduces a kind of radical inequality that forces us to pause: you have to take off your sandals, you can't enter with them on. And so I escaped the union and party parables (when a pledge starts to be taxed, it has already lost its meaning) and went on to experience the dance of affective alliances, which involves me and a constellation of people and beings through which I disappear: I no longer need to be a political entity. I can just be a person in flux, capable of making affective bonds and meanings. This is the only way to conjugate "worlding," the verb that expresses the power to experience other worlds, which opens up to other cosmovisions and manages to imagine pluriverses. These terms, used by Alberto Acosta and other Andean thinkers, evoke the possibility of worlds that affect each other, of experiencing the encounter with the mountain not as an abstraction, but as an affective dynamic in which the mountain is not only a subject, but can also take the initiative to engage with anyone. After all, this other possible "we" disrupts the centrality of the human. Not all existences can be defined by anthropocentrism, which marks, names, categorizes, and classifies everything – including others, similar ones, that are also considered less than human.

This human desire for the world has always been part of humanity, including in the ways it has characterized the colonization of entire continents. When this desire is associated with Western logic, it conveys the idea that culture is opposed to nature. The attempts at dialogue that we've heard of – for example, after the Catholic kings and the Pope put an end to the last sultan on the Iberian Peninsula back in 1400 or 1500 and began looking for new bodies to colonize – clearly show how each one was talking about a place that would have been impossible for the other to recognize. Take, for example, the statement attributed to Chief Seattle to an armed representative of the government of Washington:

> I know you came here and took over everything; your God probably made you the new owner and now you will have control over all these things, but teach your children to tread lightly on the earth, teach them to love that mountain breeze and recognize the flight of the eagle, because if you don't learn this, one day you will wake up drowning in your own vomit.[60]

[60] *TR*. As mentioned in footnote 22, it is uncertain when Chief Seattle used the word "vomit." His original speech was transcribed from notes taken by Dr. Henry Smith on October 29, 1887 in the *Seattle Sunday Star*. Smith's account, titled "Address by Chief Seattle" (see *The Hudson Review*, 23/3 (1970): 492–94), is generally believed to be mostly accurate (see Arnold Krupat, "Chief Seattle's speech revisited," *American Indian Quarterly*, 35/2 (2011): 192–214). However, over time, the speech has undergone embellishments, manipulations, and appropriations, with the addition of environmental themes not present in the "original" version published by Smith. These alterations have sentimentalized and changed the main message of the speech. This phenomenon can be observed in the work of William Arrowsmith in 1969, Ted Perry in 1971, and the 1974 version presented at the Spokane Expo. Numerous articles and books have been written about these romanticized versions of Chief

This is exactly what colonial thought has produced. The Anthropocene is amassing so much garbage, so much damage, that it has made the world sick. That's why, despite having escaped the politics of the *polis*, I've been excitedly following what's happening in Chile, following a debate already unfolding in other Andean countries from Ecuador to Bolivia. They are discussing remodeling the nation based on a plurinational state, and Elisa Loncón, a Mapuche woman, is the president-elect of the Constituent Assembly in Chile, a country that is historically very authoritarian and resistant to any kind of globalization.

But you must be careful and strong. Common sense considers democracy to be something you can put on and then walk away with – but it's not like that. In Chile itself, when Salvador Allende was president, the government palace was bombed. In the United States, the largest democracy in the world, a policeman puts his knee on a Black man's neck and suffocates him to death, while at the same time the country exports "democracy" to Lebanon, Iraq, Iran, Afghanistan. Because democracy flows there: Americans have something to provide and

---

Seattle's speech, arguing that they perpetuate stereotypes and myths about Indigenous peoples (see Albert Furtwangler, *Answering Chief Seattle*. University of Washington Press, 2011). The translators are grateful to one of the anonymous readers of this translation for sharing these references.

sell. I think we have to stop using such expressions so loosely. A banner that says "Welcome to democracy" is just crap. You'll walk in and get punched in the face. The poets say that democracy is a utopia, something that is pursued rather than consumed. Democracy is a challenge that a given society exercises as a daily practice. Just like the idea of freedom, of a people's integrity, democracy must constantly be constructed. It doesn't have the power to rest on its laurels; it is subject to all kinds of attacks.

Meanwhile, in Brazil in the 2020s, a surprising process of identity denialism takes place.[61] Imposed by colonialism, the very symbols of the nation, such as the national flag (an identity's bastion in any republic), were appropriated by such an authoritarian group of people that others were prevented

---

[61] *TR.* The recrudescence of far-right ideologies in Brazil during the 2020s has had profound consequences, including the denial and erasure of identities. This phenomenon is particularly notable in the context of marginalized communities, such as Indigenous peoples, Afro-Brazilians, LGBTQ+ individuals, and people from the Brazilian northeast. This has fueled a discourse that undermines and denies the existence and rights of these marginalized communities. It reinforces a narrow and exclusionary vision of Brazilian identity, often rooted in nationalist and ethnocentric narratives. This denialism serves to marginalize and silence these communities, further exacerbating social divisions, multiplying harmful stereotypes, and generating a climate of intolerance and discrimination.

from sharing those symbols. We're dealing with a club that has a special appreciation for guns, an array of prejudices and all sorts of fundamentalisms. Would this privatization of patriotic symbols be a new capitalist scandal? A good way to confront them is by questioning colonial truth: "My homeland, my language." Caetano Veloso[62] has a song that goes, "A língua é minha pátria / E eu não tenho pátria, tenho mátria / E quero frátria" ["Language is my fatherland / But I have no land. I have a motherland / And I want a sisterland"]. So, since Quechua is a language that exceeds the nation-state: long live La Pacha Mama and down with nationalism! *Estamos cambiando, hay que cambiar el mundo*: even if democracy has its limits, it is one of the available means of effecting change.

It's essential for us to reform our country and also to develop the idea of a plurinational state, because this old colonial state of ours has the DNA of a pirate, of a *bandeirante*: it's here to eat others. I'm still shocked that most political leaders, not only in Brazil, but on a large part of the planet, are

---

[62] *TR.* Caetano Veloso (b. 1942) is a highly influential Brazilian musician, singer, songwriter, and cultural icon. In the late 1960s, he co-founded Tropicália, a cultural and musical avant-garde movement in Brazil. His artistic legacy has left an indelible mark on Brazilian music, making him one of the most respected and influential musicians of his generation.

so alienated that they don't realize that if we don't open ourselves up to this vast cultural matrix, we'll just deepen the disaster we're already mixed up in, including from an environmental perspective. The idea of these nation-states is very poor and limited, and we have to be able to get through all this and come together. Who knows, starting from the Andes, perhaps the presence of Indigenous peoples in constructing Latin America's new constitutionalism[63] will bring other perspectives to bear on what we call "country" and "nation"? Because the native people have other contributions to this debate, both about the *polis* and about ideas of nature, ecology, and culture. If we're able to open ourselves up to this abundance, political activity will just be one more dimension of existence and not a predatory profession, as it has been for many politicians of the twenty-first century, the century of neoliberalism, whose invention has served only to subjugate bodies and enforce servitude. To escape from servitude is also to be open to the idea of occupying spaces, including the space of politics and the state, and I hope that we can help breathe new life into these environments as much as possible, as well as our rivers, which generously

[63] *TR.* The mention of Latin American constitutionalism alludes to the waves of democratization that resulted in efforts to safeguard Indigenous rights within constitutional frameworks.

flow together and share their power. May we learn to resist getting stuck in any dam. For this reason, without forgetting the dear Zapatistas, who have always inspired important debates in Latin America, before crying "¡Viva Zapata!" I cry "*Abya Yala!*" which is how our relatives greet the land and the sky in Kuna.

The Heart in the Rhythm of
the Earth

When thinking about the relationship between
education and the future, I stumble into ambiguity.
In conversations with educators from different
cultures – not only native educators, but those with
alternative approaches to childhood – I've noticed
that even in the earliest stage of life an entire
apparatus of pedagogical resources is mobilized
to shape people. This makes me think of ancient
practices of forming collectives that different peoples
on this American continent perform. These practices
are connected to the *construction* of a person,
which is very different from shaping someone. Such
practices recognize that we all share transcendence
and, when we arrive in the world, we already *are*
– and *being* is the essence of everything. The other
skills we can develop (like owning things, having a
career, ruling the world) are layers that you add to

the perspective of a being that already exists. This ancient concept is very convenient, since it doesn't clash with the experience of existing.

The Guarani perform a baptism, the *Nhemongaraí*, which takes place in their New Year, around January 25. In this ritual, inside the *opy* (the ceremonial house), the shaman sings and blows smoke on the young children, who are on their mothers' laps. The shaman keeps blowing the smoke and watching them to identify who these beings are that have arrived. After the chants have been performed, the shaman approaches the relatives and asks for the children's names. From then on, they are named as such. This beautiful ritual conveys the message that, when we enter this world, we are already complete beings. It's deeply respectful to say: this being already exists, this being doesn't need a mold; rather, it's this being that gives us the mold of who it is that has come into this world.

When we make moves to change the original design of a being, whether human or nonhuman, and mold it so that it has some use, we are committing violence against the path that it is already able to follow here on Earth. There's a song I really like to quote, which goes like this:

Singing, dancing
Flying over the fire,
We follow along a continuum,
In the wake of our ancestors.

This ancestral invocation is instructive. It produces a poetic image based on a very ancient rite: the consecration of fire. Once the wood was no longer ablaze, people were able to walk barefoot over the embers without burning their feet. It looked like magic, like an optical illusion, but it wasn't. Young folks, old folks, women, and men were able to come out on the other side without getting burned. Along the way, if the person who took part in this ritual was afraid, they would undoubtedly burn their feet and run away. Let's imagine this parable as something you've inherited, and that therefore doesn't scare you. On the contrary, it's comforting. This is a very instructive image for us to start thinking about education and the future.

First of all, the future doesn't exist – we just imagine it. To say that something is going to happen in the future doesn't require anything, for it is an illusion. So you can deposit everything there like in a game of dice. Unfortunately, from modernity onward, we have been induced into being part of the world in a competitive way. And this competitiveness, which has strengthened over centuries, ended up producing a world of gamers. If the future works out: "Bingo!" But the truth is that we are increasingly imagining the projection of very improbable futures, even though we continue to prefer this lie over and against the present.

By focusing on a potential future, we end up constructing precisely what Chimamanda Ngozi Adichie recommends that we avoid: a world with a single story.[64] Imagining such a future is very risky, as it comes encased in anxiety, rage, and a harrowing acceleration of time. Always looking to the future rather than to what is around us is directly linked to the psychological suffering that has plagued so many people, including the young. It's an experience that penetrates every pore and reflects our emotional state. The vast ecosystem of planet Earth is also suffering from the stress of this acceleration.

Nevertheless, this acceleration is real. Many scientists are looking at the way children experience childhood. Some studies show that in the last thirty or forty years, this period has become shorter. Instead of experiencing childhood as a comfortable place, children are falling into it as if it were a hotplate, where they are forced to face up to questions about an eroding world. When you talk to an adult who was a kid in the 1990s, they often speak of it as an extremely narrow period, a hallway. And if this is what a thirty-year-old says, then, if we're not careful, the next generation will have their experience of childhood – that fantastic

---

[64] *TR.* Ailton is referring to Adichie's viral TED Talk "The Danger of a Single Story" (2009).

position from which a being lands on Earth – suppressed for good and they will be confronted by a world in crisis right from the start.

In anthroposophy, the first septennium of life is considered the period in which people are still half angel, half human – not quite firmly on Earth. In the past, the most traditional people said that children under the age of seven were more susceptible to death because their souls weren't yet fully anchored, and they could take off like birds. According to these cultures, during this period, we should not be subjected to being shaped in any form. I think of the words "mold," "shape," "form," "format," etc., and that applying these concepts to people in their earliest moments of life, when they are original beings and full of subjectivity, is highly violent. These words prune spirits that could bring a lot of novelty to the Earth. Instead of *producing* a future, we should welcome this inventiveness that emerges through new people. In any culture, children are the bearers of good tidings. Instead of thinking of them as empty packages that need to be filled, jammed with information, we should consider how creativity and subjectivity emerge as capable of inventing other worlds – this is much more interesting than inventing futures.

These early years of existence chart the world and provide a type of map for adult experience. Therefore, if we don't recognize the paths during this time, then we'll walk around the world as if it were a foreign place – not only from a geographic and climatic point of view, but also as a place shared with other beings. Our sociability has to be rethought beyond human beings. It has to include bees, armadillos, whales, dolphins. My main mentors in life are a constellation of beings – human and nonhuman.

When I was eight or nine years old, I was out in the yard (a place I really like), where there was a beautiful wild mare that my brother owned. She ate corn while I raked the yard. While the mare was gnawing on the cobs, I raked close to her and unintentionally startled her. She gave me a good kick that got me in the stomach and sent me flying some three meters or so. I couldn't breathe, but soon recovered. And there, in a totally timeless way, as if it were a bolt of lightning, I learned a lesson about limits, and at the same time I realized that we can act on the world. It was a revelation that came to me like a mantra: "Yes, we can do a lot, but not everything." This is something I learned in friction with nature.

In childhood, the freedom I had to experience a connection with everything we perceive as nature helped me understand that I am also part of it. So the first gift I got from this freedom was to merge myself with nature in a general sense, to understand myself as an extension of everything, and to experience being a collective subject. I'm talking about sensing life in other beings: in a tree, in a mountain, in a fish, in a bird, and getting involved. The presence of other beings not only adds to the landscape of the place where I live, but also transforms the world. This power of perceiving oneself as belonging to a whole and being able to transform the world could be a good idea for education – not transforming the world into an imaginary time and place, but to where we are now.

Beyond where each of us is born – a place, a village, a community, a city – we are all located in a larger organism, which is the Earth. This is why we say that we are children of the Earth. This Mother forms the first layer, the womb of conscious experience, which is neither industrious nor utilitarian. I'm not talking about a guidebook to life, but a relationship inextricable from an origin, from the memory of the creation of the world and from the most comforting stories that each culture is capable of producing. In some literature, these stories are called myths. Mythologies are alive. They continue to exist whenever a community insists on inhabiting this poetic site of affective life, despite other harsh ways of narrating the world. This may not have a very practical meaning in terms of competing with others in a world in crisis, but it makes total sense in valuing life as a gift.

There's nothing more important than life. Faced
with crises and pandemics, we're going through
a collective experience of anxiety, but sensitive
states of mind also lead to resilience, the ability to
continue creating a world less susceptible to the
psychological terrorism that has hit contemporary
life. Western families in an urban context value
the education system too much. These are adults
who subscribe to the format where folks who come
into being are integrated into the world. Before
they are able to choose the experience of becoming
embedded in the world in a collective sense, they are
already raised with the adult vision of it. A twenty-
year-old youth already has a world formed within
him, and, when he adds a child into that world,
he starts acting according to his aspiration for
perfection, with the idea of forming a super subject.
That way, from early on, we start suggesting to
children that they need to reach a certain degree of
excellence and occupy prominent places, because
only one person can fit at the top of the podium.
However, this podium is a lie, because there is no
place in the world where only one person can fit;
everyone always fits.

In conflict with this way of thinking, we're seeing
young people everywhere feeling expelled from
the world. We should pay more attention to Greta
Thunberg's campaign in Europe, which pushes
young people to rebel against the adult world, and

suggests that they shouldn't go to classes that week, because, after all, school isn't that important.[65] We should take a good look at this gesture, listen to the voice of this child who hasn't given up on the world yet, and who is capable of proposing another narrative for it, because the one we've had so far needs to be questioned. Choosing another world can be accomplished here and now and it'll be done by children, not by adults. Greta's generation literally accuses adults of stealing the future. Is there a more terrible accusation than that? Education has nothing to do with the future. After all, the future is imaginary, and education is an experience that has to be real.

From now on, when we talk about education, let's consider how to associate it not with the future, but with the here and now. In Tibet and among other Middle Eastern and Asian peoples, meditation and mindfulness are educational resources. As a child, the Dalai Lama was granted a vast experiential freedom so that he could become a holistic being. Afterward, he had to flee his country; things changed, but his childhood formed his being. I'm giving an example that is well known around the world, but thousands of other children of

[65] *TR*. Krenak's interpretation of Greta Thunberg's activism conveys his idea that schools aren't as significant as the ecological education with which humanity should be engaging.

his generation and of previous generations were encouraged and sheltered in this way so that they experienced childhood as the foundation of life. And they were happy to be part of a culture where this is a collective practice.

In the West, this is not a prevailing practice. Quite the contrary, making people conform has always been the imperative of the education we're familiar with. The classroom already conveys this by assembling children of the same age group, who are then supervised by an adult, the teacher. This very clearly illustrates the external intervention made on each person. They lose their autonomy and begin to feel compelled to align themselves with a standardized way of thinking. But what if we suggest that children start to have time for themselves, that educational experience is converted into a shelter for this period so that a person becomes self-determining, instead of being externally shaped?

In order to foster and facilitate an experience that includes less molding and more invention, we need to start a revolution from the perspective of the established standards in institutionalized education, as well as in the choices that families make. If we take a sample of two hundred families and say to them: "Would you be willing to release your child in the next five, six years from any standardizing and encourage a playful experience with water, with the river, with earth, with fire, with everything, to be an element of global transition, of changing the global mindset?" – maybe twenty would agree.

The truth is that children of seven or eight years old are already starting to be trained to ignore the environment. They are isolated in a classroom to learn how to read and write and, from an early age, the idea of a sanitary life is instilled in them. (This is very contradictory, because many children in urban communities don't even have access to basic hygiene, but they are quickly taught to be disgusted with the Earth.) What I call "sanitary education" occurs much earlier than the norms prescribed by the COVID-19 pandemic. It's the gradual formation, over decades, of a mindset in which children are discouraged from touching earth so as not to get their hands dirty, that if you pull a potato out of the ground, you shouldn't bring it into the house because it's dirty. (Ideally, get a rinsed and packaged potato from the supermarket.) When did earth become dirt? I've been seeing this sanitary blitz in children's heads for a while now, and I haven't seen any educators questioning it. So, for me, this mindset is directly connected to this way of seeing the world as a warehouse, and it lies at the core of the environmental crisis we are facing today.

I referenced meditation because it enables people to ground themselves in the present. Who knows, maybe this practice should be tried out in all schools? Since it won't be easy to pull children out of academic settings and send them into nature to experience direct contact with the Earth, let's at least provide a safe space for them to contemplate their own thoughts – which are undoubtedly luminous, arriving in the world bearing wonders – without bombarding them with arguments. Children can then creatively and positively associate themselves with these beautiful thoughts and become the bearers of ancestry here on Earth: a present brought to us by newcomers.

I was happy to learn that, in his remarks about education, Pope Francis mentioned invoking our ancestors. To the vast gathering of youth that was listening, he emphasized the need to reconnect with our ancestry. I found this to be marvelous, since it's not very typical of a pope's address and the idea was abandoned in the twentieth century as if it were an attribute of old and "primitive" cultures. When the Pope said that this is an essential value for facing the crises we are experiencing today, I was filled with joy, as it contributes to dismantling cultural and racial borders so that people can speak in a more respectful way about cultural diversity and the plurality of life. These ideas should guide the entire educational curriculum.

Unfortunately, educational policy in Brazil sees school as a mere building, and that is why the work of educators is so devalued. The room is filled with children and the door is locked: that's it, they're at school now. This place can even signify a family's abandonment of their responsibility in their children's education. Many children are so deprived of guidance by their collective nuclear family that at a certain point they aren't able to talk to their parents anymore. They're kidnapped by the educational system and there is no longer a common language left between them.

Since the late 1990s, there has been a program in Brazil that has been largely consolidated since the early 2000s: the *Plano Nacional de Educação Escolar Indígena* (National Plan for Indigenous Education).[66] It is a specialized form of education implemented in Indigenous territories all over Brazil, where each community has the freedom to design schooling according to their preferences. I have already been present at a school in a village under a tree and I thought it was very good. People were comfortable with that experience and didn't need any buildings. After a while, those children decided it would be good to have a classroom, but they also know that pedagogical experience can be achieved on the banks of a stream, on a slab

---

[66] TR. The *Plano Nacional de Educação Escolar Indígena* is a government initiative that was established to address the specific educational needs and cultural rights of Indigenous peoples in Brazil.

of stone, anywhere. It's a group effort to make a collective investigation. Even literacy itself can do well without a classroom. School is not just a building; it's an intergenerational exchange that should be enhanced and valued, in which people who have gone through different things can share matters that help children prepare for adult life.

Some Indigenous schools – in struggling through attempts to reconfigure the system – try to stay as close as possible to what I am arguing for, seeking to prepare each student in the context of their community, to take action there. These schools are not launching pads for children, but places for them to be. We who persist in collective experience do not educate children to be the winners of something, but to be each other's companions. For example, we do not aim for them to become bosses. We don't train people to be in charge of others. The foundations of education are constructed in friction with everyday life. A child's eventual leadership will be the result of the daily experience of collaborating with others, not competing with them.

That boy I was never stops being close by to talk, to amuse me, to do something new. He passes by his fishing basket on the riverbank knowing that there might be a snake there, but he doesn't stop: that's courage. The friction with life generates a field of subjectivity that prepares a person for any task. Instead of shaping someone to be something, we should first think about the possibility of providing experiences that form people capable of achieving everything that is necessary in life: without fear of a snake in the water or of being kicked. Because all of this is implicit, these are fundamental experiences for perceiving oneself as part of a collective subject, for learning that we are not alone in the world.

Krenak children long to be ancient. This is because among human communities in which children still have the freedom and autonomy to long for worlds, they really value their elders. The elders gain perspective from various stages of life experience. They are the storytellers, those who teach the study of medicine, art, the foundations of everything relevant to having a good life. This is what the Quechua people call *"sumak kawsay"*[67] and which has been translated into Spanish as *"bienvivir,"* or *"bem viver"* in Portuguese. I believe that our children know about the subjective psychological security that this experience can provide, and that is why they do not see aging as a threat, but as a coveted site of knowledge, which questions the hypothesis of shaping people for another world,

---

[67] *TR. "Sumak kawsay,"* which translates literally to "good living" or more figuratively to suggest "the plentiful life," is a Quechua phrase that emerged in the 1990s to describe a political project that honors Quechua ancestral knowledge and cultural values. As an anticapitalist paradigm, it seeks the collective wellbeing of peoples in relation to nature.

rather than the place where each of us experiences day-to-day life.

Indigenous children are not educated, but guided. They don't learn to be winners, because for some to win, others need to lose. They learn to share the place where they live and what they have to eat. They learn from the model of a life in which the individual counts less than the collective. This is the Indigenous wisdom, a legacy that passes from generation to generation. What our children learn from early on is to put their hearts in the rhythm of the Earth.

An Oraliture[68] of Encounter

I consider it timely for us to examine the process of crafting Ailton Krenak's books, especially *Life Is Not Useful* and this more recent volume you now hold, *Ancestral Future*. Ailton's words have found rich soil in a collapsing world predominantly governed by productivism. By shedding light on this alternative literary endeavor, my aim is to contribute, to some extent, to the dehierarchization of knowledge production – challenging the

[68] *TR.* The term "oraliture" has diverse genealogies and itineraries across the Americas. In *Le Discours antillais* (1981), Édouard Glissant notes that this neologism was coined by Haitian intellectuals to supplant the term "literature" and to emphasize oral traditions. In *Afrografias da Memória* (1997) Leda Maria Martins describes *"oralitura"* as encompassing the fabric of oral and physical performances, serving as a conduit for the transmission of memory and history beyond writing and through corporeal expression.

overemphasis on academic thought at the expense of other epistemologies that are so desirable and increasingly indispensable. Here as well, we present readers with words captured mid-flight, tracing diverse trajectories before they settle on the page.

Ailton's literature is born, above all, from the spoken word, but it goes beyond that. It emerges from a practice of encounter. Those who have heard him speak live know: his interventions are porous, alive, nourished by his interlocutors, the environment in which they are spoken, and the surroundings. His thinking also happens through the body. Ailton never prepares a speech – he prepares himself for it. Upon hearing a question, he usually brings his knees together, rests his hands on his thighs, and closes his eyes for a moment. His body concentrates, and his mind expands. Who is asking the questions? What are they asking? Where on the planet are we? Which recent or past political events have shaped the context we find ourselves in? Are we within four walls, or is there wind, a horizon, other presences sharing this moment with us? And so, with purpose, carrying what was and what is – and perhaps what will be – he draws his bow taut to launch his arrows. His public appearances often contain good doses of irony, some hints of acidity, the clash of different realities, and substantial amounts of lucidity, patience, and generosity.

My work in this partnership has been to observe Ailton's public interventions, whether virtual or in person, and to follow the thread of his ideas, selecting and relating excerpts, recognizing recurring images and how they evolve, grouping them into families, putting them in friction with each other, tracking their maturation and renewal over the years – and even decades – and with this sophisticated organic material, to weave the texts and compose the volumes presented to the public. Furthermore, my work is to propose their sequence, titles, epigraphs, and whatever else is necessary and welcomed to fit them onto the pages. It is a matter of gathering with one's hands some of this flowing water that is Ailton's living thinking in order to provide something for readers to drink, taking the utmost care to maintain its freshness, without an inappropriate domestication of the language often imposed by the written word and the production of books.

Language[69] rebels in Ailton's mouth. Portuguese, the language imposed by the colonizer, here translated into English, is the breeding ground for his ideas, but it also remains a language of erasure. It remains the language of eradication and mistreatment of so many Indigenous languages

---

[69] *TR*. The Portuguese word here is "*língua*," which means both "tongue" and "language."

and their speakers – including the Krenak – that covered and still covers this piece of land that some called Brazil. We know that epistemological violence has a special preference for the realm of language. Ailton does not shy away from this fight: he conjugates subjects, restores subjectivity to rivers and mountains, sows new words, turns old words inside out, and borrows words from other Indigenous relatives and their knowledges. In order for it to fit other ways of narrating the world, sometimes this tongue needs to be twisted. And part of the mission I gave myself is to tend to this lexical subversion, which the poets know so well. Let the ambiguities, intentional dissonances and novelties enacted by the author's utterances span across the printed pages. (And here, I challenge translators to join us.) I even believe this is one of the reasons for the success of Ailton's books: whoever reads them finds, beyond the power of his ideas, a text that allows itself to be unusual, poetic, brazen, provocative, cultured, and colloquial in its own way. The idea is to bring readers as close as possible to *the Ailtonian experience.*

Time is an ally in this task, as is being close to Ailton for a good part of his journey and being familiar with his voice, which I seek to preserve on paper. Alongside this is my own craft as a writer and, moreover, acknowledging the connections that give rise to his thinking. Indeed, Ailton's observations are inseparably linked to the whole tradition of Amerindian thought. As he himself says when referring to his comrades: "We walk in constellation." There is an understanding shared by many diverse peoples that at the heart of life is abundance, celebration, the commons, and maintaining balance between spiritual and material life with relationships that aren't mediated by money or captured by the abstract idea of private property. Ailton is the son and grandson of those who came before him – his ancestors – for whom the land does not belong to us. We belong to it.

Even though I'm not Indigenous, I've been lucky to be close to Indigenous people (both urban and village people) of diverse communities since I was born. I move and I keep moving through various material and symbolic territories in which the ideas Ailton evokes are experienced in the flesh. So hearing about them doesn't pull the rug out from under me: these ideas are a place I return to with joy, which revives a healthier and more meaningful world order in me. Ours is also an encounter extended in time and space. It is with equal joy that I have seen, with my hands full of earth, Ailton's words sprouting across five continents. In addition to having become a representative of a certain way of perceiving our place on the planet, and of reconsidering the centrality of humanity and even its conceptual unity, Ailton dialogues with, as well as cites and summons, thinkers, scientists, poets, musicians, and other well-known people from the most diverse traditions with the respect and fluidity of the great intellectual and avid reader that he is.

It has been an honor for me to join this journey, enjoying this space of trust that emerges from giving form to these free books – books spreading in flocks, which, as part of a larger movement, have collaborated in reforesting imaginaries on this planet, where the idea of monoculture has spread like a plague over the last few centuries. *Ancestral Future* is the new seed we sow in this field, with the belief that an idea, when it finds its time, can only flourish.

Rita Carelli

Editorial Note

Ancestral Future was edited and collated with supplemental research by Rita Carelli based on Ailton Krenak's participation in the following events:

- Cosmic politics – Opening dialogue at the Festival Seres Rios, with Ailton Krenak and Marisol de la Cadena and moderated by Ana Gomes, in August 2021.
- Rivers and cities – Talk-performance with Ailton Krenak, in the second edition of *Amazônia das Palavras*, in November 2021.
- Cartographies to postpone the end of the world – FLIP (International Literary Festival of Paraty) online panel, with Ailton Krenak and Muniz Sodré and moderated by Vagner Amaro, in December 2021.

- Spaces to breathe – XV Seminário Internacional da Escola da Cidade, with Ailton Krenak and Wellington Cançado and moderated by Francisco Fanucci, in August 2020.
- Interview for UOL (Universo Online) online media: Ailton Krenak, Indigenous leader – Ailton Krenak interviewed by Fabiola Cidral, Leonardo Sakamoto, and Maria Carolina Trevisan, in November 2021.
- Life is not useful – Live streaming from TV channel 26 and HD channel 526 on Net-Rio, with Ailton Krenak and interviewer Rosangela Coelho, in August 2020.
- Time and education: The importance of ancestral knowledge – Speech by Ailton Krenak at the Second Virtual Book Congress, in October 2020.

About the Author

Ailton Krenak was born in 1953 in the Doce River valley region, a territory of the Krenak people and a place whose ecology has been severely impacted by mining. An activist in the socioenvironmental movement and in defense of Indigenous rights, he organized the Aliança dos Povos da Floresta (Alliance of Forest Peoples), which unites riverine and Indigenous communities in the Amazon. He is one of the most prominent leaders of the movement that emerged from the Indigenous Awakening in the 1970s in Brazil, and he also contributed to the creation of the Union of Indigenous Nations (UNI). Ailton has done extensive educational and environmental work as a journalist and in video and television programs. His struggles in the 1970s and 1980s were decisive for the inclusion of the chapter on Indigenous rights in the 1988 Brazilian

Constitution, which guaranteed Indigenous rights to ancestral homelands and culture, at least on paper. He is the co-author of the UNESCO proposal that created the Serra do Espinhaço Biosphere Reserve in 2005 and is a member of its managing committee. He was awarded the Order of Cultural Merit of the Presidency of the Republic, and in 2016 he was awarded an honorary doctorate from the Federal University of Juiz de Fora in Minas Gerais. He is also the author of *Ideas to Postpone the End of the World* (House of Anansi Press, 2019) and *Life Is Not Useful* (Polity, 2023).